Emily's Bag

I Talk You Talk Press

CONTENTS

I Talk You Talk Press

CHAPTER ONE

Nina is in her car. It is 4:10pm. She is driving home from work. She works part-time in a pizza restaurant. She is tired. Many customers came to the restaurant for lunch today. The traffic light changes to red. She stops. It is raining heavily. She looks out of the side window. There is a very big shopping centre with a big car park. She sees an old woman standing next to the road. The woman doesn't have an umbrella. She is carrying a large shopping bag.

That bag looks heavy, thinks Nina. *Is the woman waiting for someone? Is she OK?* The traffic lights change to green. Nina turns the corner and stops her car. She gets out of her car and walks to the old woman.

"Excuse me, are you OK?"

The old woman looks at her.

"I'm tired," says the old woman.

"Are you waiting for someone?" asks Nina.

"No, I'm walking home, but my bag is very heavy. I'm taking a rest," says the woman.

"But it is raining! Where do you live?"

"I live in Devon Street," says the woman.

"I know Devon Street," says Nina. "I can take you there."

The old woman smiles at Nina. "Is that OK? You are very kind."

Nina smiles. "Of course it is OK. You can't walk to Devon Street in the rain with your heavy bag."

"Thank you so much." The old woman and Nina walk to Nina's car. Nina opens the door for the old woman and the woman gets into the car slowly. Then Nina closes the door and walks around the car to the driver's side. She gets in and closes the door.

"The rain is so heavy!" says Nina. "We are very wet!"

Nina starts to drive. "If you walk to Devon Street, it will take you fifteen minutes," says Nina. "It will take only five minutes by car."

Nina looks at the woman's bag. "Have you been shopping?" she asks.

"Yes," says the woman.

"Do you go shopping every day?" asks Nina.

"I go most days."

"And do you walk to Devon Street every day?"

"Yes. Before, I got the bus. But the bus services changed, and now, no buses go near Devon Street."

"Do you live alone?" asks Nina.

"Yes," says the old woman.

"Do you have family? A son or daughter? They can help you with your shopping."

The woman is quiet for a few seconds. Then she says, "No, my husband died, and I don't have any children." Nina looks at her. The woman looks sad, so Nina doesn't ask any more questions.

"Where do you live?" asks the old woman.

"I live on Church Street," says Nina.

"Oh, that is not far from Devon Street," says the old woman. "What's your name?"

"I'm Nina."

"I'm Emily," says the old woman.

Nina drives into Devon Street. "Which house is yours?"

"Oh, please stop here. I can walk to my house. Devon Street is narrow, and there are many cars parked at the sides of the road."

"OK," says Nina. She stops the car.

Thank you, Nina. You are very kind," says Emily.

"You're welcome Emily. When you get home, have a nice cup of tea and put your heater on."

Emily smiles. "Of course. I need a hot cup of tea." She gets out of the car and walks slowly down the road.

That bag looks very heavy, thinks Nina.

CHAPTER TWO

Nina goes home. Her daughter and son are back from school. Her daughter, Libby, is 14. She is sitting on the sofa, doing her homework. Her son, James, is 16. He is playing a computer game on the TV.

"How was your day?" asks Nina.

"It was good," says Libby. "But we got wet walking home in the rain."

"How was your day, mum?" asks James.

"It was hard. We had many customers at lunchtime. But after that, I met an old woman. Her name is Emily. She was walking home to Devon Street in the rain. She didn't have an umbrella. So, I took her home. She had a very big shopping bag. It looked very heavy."

"That's nice of you," says Libby. "But why didn't Emily take the bus?"

"The bus system changed. So now, no buses go near Devon Street."

"How about a taxi?" asks James.

Nina thinks about it. "I don't think Emily has much money. Her coat was old. Her shoes were old."

"But she had a big shopping bag. So she bought many things," says James.

"Yes, that's strange," says Nina. "But maybe she bought potatoes or milk. OK, I'm going to start making dinner soon, but first, I need a cup of tea."

Nina goes into the kitchen and puts the kettle on.

What can I cook tonight? she thinks. *I can make chicken pie and potatoes.*

The children like my chicken pie.

Nina doesn't have a husband. She is a single mother. She works hard at the restaurant every day. She doesn't like her job, but she needs the money. James and Libby want to go to university when they are older.

She makes a cup of tea and goes back into the living room. She sits on a chair and relaxes. It was a long day.

CHAPTER THREE

The next day, Nina works hard in the restaurant. At 4:00pm, she says 'goodbye' to the other staff members and walks to her car. It is not raining today, but it is cloudy. She gets in her car and drives through the town. It is a small town, but there is a department store, and a very large shop. The shop is called We Have Everything!

We Have Everything! sells many items – food, clothes, DVDs, jewellery, kitchen items, and many other things. Nina stops at the traffic lights next to We Have Everything!

"Oh!" she says. She is very surprised. Emily is standing at the side of the road.

"It's Emily!" Nina turns left and stops her car. She gets out.

"Emily!" she shouts.

Emily turns around. "Oh, Nina! Hello! Thank you for yesterday."

"Are you going home?" asks Nina.

"Yes, I'm walking home."

"Come on, I'll take you," says Nina.

Nina looks at Emily's bag. It is very big and looks heavy. *Did she go shopping again?* she thinks. *Yesterday she had a big, heavy shopping bag. Today she has a big, heavy shopping bag. Why? She has no family. Why does she need so much shopping?*

Emily walks to Nina's car. "Oh you are so kind," she says. Emily gets in the car. She puts the shopping bag between her feet. Nina wants to look inside the shopping bag, but she thinks it is rude, so she doesn't look.

"Have you been shopping again, Emily?" she asks.

"Yes, I needed a few things," says Emily.

Then Nina thinks, *Many old people are lonely. They go shopping every day so they can meet people. Some old people like to buy many things. They keep the things in their houses. Maybe Emily is like that. I shouldn't ask questions about her shopping.*

"The weather is better today," says Nina.

"Yes, it is. It isn't raining today," says Emily. "Do you have children?"

"Yes, I have a son and a daughter," says Nina. "My son is sixteen, and my daughter is fourteen."

Emily smiles. "That's nice. What's your husband's job?"

"I don't have a husband," says Nina.

"Oh, I'm sorry," says Emily.

Nina smiles. "It's OK. I'm happy with my two children."

"Are they good children?" asks Emily.

"Very good," says Nina. "They study hard. In the future, James wants to be a policeman, and Libby wants to be a teacher."

Emily smiles. "You are lucky. You have two nice children."

Nina stops the car at the top of Devon Street. "Is here OK?" she asks.

"Oh yes. Thank you very much. You are very kind."

Emily gets out of the car, but it is difficult because her bag is so heavy.

"Do you need any help?" asks Nina.

"Oh no, I'm fine," says Emily. "Thank you."

She closes the door. Nina watches her walk down the street. She is very surprised. Emily doesn't go into a house on Devon Street. She turns a corner and walks into the next street.

That's strange, thinks Nina. *Maybe she is going to see her friend before she goes home. Maybe some of the shopping is for a friend. Maybe her friend is very old and can't go into town.*

Nina drives home.

Every day is the same. Nina finishes work at 4:00pm and drives through the town. Every day, she sees Emily waiting next to the road at the traffic lights with a big, heavy shopping bag. Every day, she stops and takes Emily home. They talk about Nina's children, and her job, but they never talk about Emily or her life. Emily becomes quiet when Nina asks her questions about her life. But Nina enjoys talking to Emily.

One day, when Nina stops at the top of Devon Street, Emily looks at Nina and says, "You are like a daughter to me." Nina wants to cry. But she thinks something is strange. Emily never goes into a house in Devon Street. She always walks to the next street. But Nina doesn't ask questions. She is happy to help Emily. But soon, everything will change...

CHAPTER FOUR

David Jones is a policeman. Now, he is at We Have Everything! The shop has a problem. Every week, the staff check the items in the store on the computer. They check the money too. Something is strange. Some items are missing. The items are DVDs, jewellery, silk ties, scarves, brand name shirts, and shoes. Yesterday, the department store asked David Jones to go to their store. They are having problems too. Some hats are missing. Their hats are expensive.

David Jones is sitting with the manager of We Have Everything! They are in the manager's office. "Someone is taking things from the store," says the manager. "They are taking them, but they are not paying for them."

"So someone is stealing things from your store," says David.

"That's right," says the manager. "We have security cameras in the store. We have recordings from last week until today. Can you check the security camera video for us?"

"Yes," says David. "It will take me a few hours, but I can check the video for you. I want to catch the bad person."

David thinks there is a bad person, or maybe two or three bad people stealing the items. The manager of We Have Everything! brings David a cup of tea, and switches on the video screen.

"Thank you," says David. "I will find the bad person for you."

The person is taking DVDs and expensive shirts and shoes. I think the bad person is a young man, he thinks.

After watching the video for three hours, David is tired, and surprised. He sees the same old woman on the video every day. She comes to the store at the same time in the afternoon, and leaves at 4:10pm. He watches her on the video carefully. She looks at ties, shoes, shirts and DVDs. She is carrying a large shopping bag. When she leaves the shop, the bag looks bigger, and heavier. The video is not so clear, so David cannot see if the woman is taking the items.

I don't think she is the bad person. She is just an old woman. But I will follow her tomorrow, he thinks. He tells the manager. The manager thinks it is a good idea.

CHAPTER FIVE

The next day, David doesn't wear his uniform. He wears a sweater and jeans. He goes into We Have Everything! at 2:30pm. He looks at socks and hats, but really, he is watching the door. At 3:00pm, the old woman comes into the shop. She looks at him, and then walks to the DVD section. David waits for a few seconds, and then walks to the DVD section too. The old woman is looking at movies. She picks up the DVDs, and reads the back of the DVD cases. She looks at David. Then, she puts the DVDs back on the rack. She walks to the tie section. David waits a few seconds and then walks to the tie section too. The woman looks at silk ties. She looks around. She sees David again, and puts the ties back on the hanger.

She is looking at me, thinks David. *She looks like a nice old lady. Is she the bad person?*

The woman goes to the plant section and looks at the plants. David walks to the car goods section. From the car goods section he can see the plant section. The woman looks at some plants, but she doesn't touch them. Soon, it is 4:10pm. The woman goes out of the shop. David waits for a few seconds, and goes out of the shop too. He watches the old woman. She walks across the car park and stands at the traffic lights. Then, a car stops. David can see a woman driving the car. The old woman walks to the car and gets into it.

Who is that? thinks David. *Is that her daughter?*

He goes back into the shop and goes to the manager's office. The manager is looking at the video.

"I watched the old woman," says David. "She didn't take

anything."

"Really?" says the manager. "I checked the ties. There are two black ties and one red tie missing. The woman is on the video. She is looking at the ties."

"But I watched her! She only looked at the ties!" says David.

"Look at this," says the manager. They watch the video carefully. "Look. The woman is holding a tie. Then, she puts the tie back on the hanger. But look, the tie goes into her bag."

David is shocked. "I didn't see that!" he says.

"The woman is very good at this," says the manager. "She practices every day."

"I will wait for her tomorrow," says David. "And I will check the other woman."

"The other woman?" asks the manager. "Who is that?"

"A woman in a car picked her up at the traffic lights," says David. "I think she is helping the old woman. Don't worry. We will catch the bad people!"

CHAPTER SIX

The next day, Nina is driving home from work. The traffic lights outside We Have Everything! are on red. She stops.

That's strange, she thinks. *Emily is not here.*

She looks around, but she can't see Emily.

Maybe she is busy today. Or maybe she is tired. I hope she is OK, thinks Nina. The traffic lights change to green, and Nina starts to drive. At the next set of traffic lights, she sees a police car behind her. The police car's blue lights are on. The policeman is flashing the lights.

Does he want me to stop? thinks Nina. *But why? I haven't done anything bad.*

She stops the car at the side of the road. The policeman stops too, and gets out of his car. He walks to Nina's car.

"Hello," says Nina.

"Good afternoon," says David. "I'd like to ask you some questions."

Nina looks at him. She is shocked. "Am I in trouble?" she asks.

"No, but I want to ask you some questions. Please come and sit in the police car."

Nina gets out of her car and walks to the police car with David. She gets in the back of the car. David sits in the driver's seat.

"I saw you pick up an old lady yesterday," says David.

"Emily! Is she OK? She wasn't waiting for me today, so I am worried," says Nina.

David looks at Nina. "Do you pick her up every day?"

"Yes. She goes shopping at We Have Everything! every day. Then,

I pick her up."

"Why? Is she a family member? Does she live near you?"

"No. One day, I was driving home. I saw her at the traffic lights. It was raining, and she had a big shopping bag. I wanted to help her. So, I took her home."

David is writing in his notebook. "Where does she live?" he asks.

"I take her to Devon Street. So I think she lives there," says Nina.

"What does she buy in We Have Everything!?" asks David.

"I don't know," says Nina. "But she always has a big, heavy bag. Why are you asking me these questions? Is Emily in trouble?"

"I can't answer your question," says David. "But, I have a question for you. Can I look in your car?"

"Of course."

David gets out of the car and walks to Nina's car.

This is strange, thinks Nina. *I don't understand.*

She sends a message on her phone to Libby and James.

--- *I will be a little late coming home today.* ---

She puts her phone in her bag and watches David. He is opening all the car doors and looking inside the car. Then, he gets into the car. After a few seconds, he gets out of the car. He is holding something.

What's that? thinks Nina. *Maybe James or Libby dropped something in my car.*

David comes back to the police car. He gets in and looks at Nina.

"What are these?" he asks.

He is holding two DVDs and a silk tie. Nina looks at them. She is very surprised.

"I don't know," she says. "Maybe Emily bought them. Maybe she dropped them."

"They were under your front car seat," says David. "Your friend Emily didn't pay for these items. She took them from We Have Everything! I think you are helping her."

"What? Wait a minute!" says Nina loudly. "Emily is taking items from a shop? She is stealing things?"

"Yes. Someone is taking things from We Have Everything! I watched the security video. Every day, Emily looks at DVDs, ties, shirts and shoes. Every day, DVDs, ties, shirts and shoes are missing."

"But Emily is a little old lady! She is not a bad person!" says Nina.

David looks at Nina. "Are you helping Emily?"

"What?" asks Nina.

"She waits for you every day. Every day she has a big, heavy shopping bag. You take her home. Are you helping her? She takes the items, and you take her and the items home."

"No, of course I'm not helping her!"

"I think it's strange," says David. "She is not your family member. She doesn't live in your street. You don't know her very well. So why do you take her home every day?"

"Because…because…I want to help her with her heavy bag. That's all," says Nina. "The first time, I took her home because it was raining, and now, I want to help her. There are no buses to Devon Street, and she always has a heavy bag. And I like her. She is nice."

"I'm going to take you to the police station. I think you and Emily are working as a team. She takes the items, and you help her to escape."

"No! That's not true!" says Nina. "You can't take me to the police station. I am not a bad person!"

David calls another police officer on his radio. Then, he says to Nina, "A police officer will drive your car to the police station. I will take you in this car. At the police station, I want you to tell us the truth!"

"But I'm telling you the truth! I'm not helping Emily to escape! I only take her home!"

David doesn't say anything. He waits for the other police officer. When she comes, he starts to drive to the police station.

Nina is very sad and angry. She wants to cry.

CHAPTER SEVEN

At the police station, David and Nina go into a small room. There is another policeman there.

"We checked every house in Devon Street on the computer," says the other policeman. "Emily doesn't live in Devon Street."

David looks at Nina. "Emily doesn't live in Devon Street. So, where does she live?"

"I don't know," says Nina.

"But you take her to Devon Street," says David. "Is that true?"

"Of course it is true."

"Which house does she go into?"

"I don't know. When she gets out of the car, I go. But she always walks to another street. Maybe she lives in the next street."

"I will check," says the other policeman. He goes out of the room.

"Can I call my children?" asks Nina. "They will be worried."

"OK," says David.

Nina calls Libby's phone.

"Libby? It's me. Are you and James OK?.....I'm sorry, but I'm going to be late....no I'm OK. But I'm at the police station.....no, I didn't have an accident. The police want to talk to me about something....don't worry, I'm fine. I'll see you later."

Nina puts her phone down on the table. "My children are worried," she says. "I am a single mother."

"I see," says David. "Where do you work?"

"In the pizza restaurant."

"So, you don't get much money. So, does Emily sell the items and share the money with you?"

"What? Of course not! You cannot say that to me!" Nina feels very angry.

The other policeman comes back into the room. "Emily doesn't live in any street near Devon Street. Is her name really Emily?"

"She said, 'My name is Emily'. So I think her name is Emily," says Nina.

"What is her last name?" asks David.

"I don't know," says Nina. She is tired and hungry. It is 6:00pm. "Can I go home now?"

"If you go home, you will contact Emily. You will tell her everything," says David.

"I won't! I don't know her phone number, or her address!" says Nina.

The other policeman says, "I will search some more." He goes out of the room.

"When can I go home?" asks Nina.

"You can go home when we find Emily," says David.

Nina wants to cry.

"I have to make dinner for my children!" she says.

Then, the other policeman comes into the room.

"We can't find her, but we found some new information. A man called Stephen Jones lives in Frank Street. Frank Street is next to Devon Street. He has been in trouble before. He took items from the department store, but didn't pay for them. Does he know Emily? We don't know. But now, a police officer will go to his house."

CHAPTER EIGHT

Twenty minutes later, another police officer and a man come into the room.

"Do you know this man?" David asks Nina.

Nina looks at the man. "No. I don't know him," she says. "Who is he?"

"Stephen Jones. Emily's son," says the other police officer.

"Who are you?" asks Stephen. He is looking at Nina, but he is not smiling. Nina thinks he looks scary.

"I am Nina. I know your mother."

"Sit down," says David.

Stephen sits down. "My mother," he says. "Is she in trouble? She is getting old. She is sometimes strange. She forgets many things. She does strange things. What happened?"

David shows Stephen the DVDs and tie.

"Oh yes," says Stephen. "My mother likes shopping."

"Your mother didn't buy these items," says David. "She took them. She didn't pay."

"So she stole them?" asks Stephen. He looks very surprised.

"Yes," says David.

"So why do you want to talk to me? Talk to my mother," says Stephen.

"Every day, Nina takes your mother to Devon Street. You live near Devon Street."

"Yes, I see my mother every day. She goes shopping. She brings me presents. She brings me DVDs and ties sometimes. She buys me food. She brings the food to my house."

"Why don't you buy your own food?" asks David. "Your mother is old."

"She likes shopping," says Stephen.

"How does she go home?" asks David. "Do you take her in your car?"

"No, she walks to her home in Park Road," says Stephen.

Nina is shocked. "But your mother is old!" she says. "Park Road is far from Devon Street!"

"Yes, but she likes walking," says Stephen.

"Why does she bring you presents?" asks David.

"Because she loves me," says Stephen. He is smiling.

"Does she bring you presents every day?"

"Not every day. But sometimes, she brings shoes or shirts."

"What do you do with them?" asks David.

"I sell them online. I don't want them," says Stephen.

A policewoman comes into the room. "Emily is here," she says. "We are asking her questions in the next room."

David stands up. "Wait here," he says, and walks out of the room.

CHAPTER NINE

David looks at Emily. He has seen her before. He saw her in We Have Everything! She looks old and tired.

"Why am I here?" she asks quietly.

"We want to talk to you," says David. "What are these?" He shows Emily the DVDs and tie.

Emily looks at them. "They are DVDs and a tie," she says.

"Did you take them?"

Emily looks at the floor. She doesn't say anything.

"Did you take them from We Have Everything!?" asks David.

"I bought them," says Emily.

"You bought them? But I watched you on the security camera. You go to We Have Everything! every day. But you don't buy anything. You look at ties, shirts, shoes and DVDs. Then, you take them. How many ties and shirts and shoes do you need? Why do you need them?"

"I like them," says Emily. She looks at the floor again.

"Do you give them to your son?" asks David.

"No, of course not," says Emily. "But, how did you get the DVDs and the tie?"

"We found them in Nina's car."

Emily looks shocked.

"Pardon?"

"We found them in Nina's car. Is she helping you?"

"Of course not! Is Nina here?"

"Yes, she is. We think she is helping you to escape."

"That's not true! Nina is a good person!"

"Why does she pick you up every day?"

"She thinks the bag is too heavy for me to carry. She is nice to me."

"We found two DVDs and a tie in her car. They are from We Have Everything! So, she is in trouble."

"Please. No. She is a good person. She didn't do anything bad," says Emily.

"Well, if you don't tell us the truth, she will be in a lot of trouble."

Emily starts to cry. "OK, I will tell you the truth. My son doesn't work. He tells me to take items from shops in town. Then, I take the items to him. He sells them on the Internet. He gets money. I don't want to do it. But he says, 'If you don't do it, I will hit you.' I am alone. My husband is dead, and I have no other children. When I said 'no', he became very angry with me. I was scared. So, I do it."

"Why does he ask you to do it?"

"Because I am an old woman. I don't look like a bad person. Security guards don't look at me. They look at young people. It is easy for me to take things."

David looks at Emily. *She is the same age as my mother,* he thinks. *She is not a bad person. She has a bad son.*

"Please wait here," he says. He goes into the other room. He looks at Nina.

"Nina, you can go home," he says.

"Really? Thank you," says Nina. She is very tired and worried about her children.

"You won't see Emily near We Have Everything! again," says David.

"What are you going to do with Emily?" asks Nina.

"Don't worry about Emily," says David. "She will be fine."

"Thank you," says Nina. She walks out of the room and closes the door. Another policeman takes her to her car. She gets in her car and drives home.

Libby and James will be worried, she thinks. *I can't believe it. I was helping an old lady, and then I had trouble. Sometimes, life is strange.*

CHAPTER TEN

David looks at Emily and Stephen.

"Stephen, we are going to search your house and your computer. We know you are selling items."

Stephen looks at his mother. "Did you tell the police?" he shouts. "Why?"

"Stop it!" says David. "Your mother is old. You should be nice to your mother. You are a very bad son. Your mother did very bad things for you, because she is scared of you. If we find items in your house, you will go to prison for a long time."

"Now I am in trouble!" shouts Stephen. "Why did you do this to me? I am your only son!"

Emily starts to cry.

"I'm sorry! But Nina was in trouble. That was not fair," she says.

"So? Who is more important to you, Nina, or me?" asks Stephen.

Emily looks at Stephen. Now she is angry. "Nina is a good person, but you are bad. You should go to prison!"

A policeman takes Stephen out of the room. "Come with me," he says. We are going to check your house."

The door closes. Emily looks at David.

"What are you going to do with me? I did a bad thing."

David looks at Emily. "Yes, you did a bad thing. But I understand your problem. Your son is bad. He is not nice to you. You are scared of him. I will take you home. Then, you can forget about this."

Emily looks at him. "Forget about it?"

"Yes, forget about it. Come on, let's go."

David takes Emily home, and then he goes back to the police station. It is late, and he is tired. He looks at the paperwork about Emily. Then, he puts it in the garbage bin.

I was tired. I lost the paperwork, he thinks.

CHAPTER ELEVEN

A few weeks later, Nina is at work. It is nearly 4:00pm and there are not many people in the restaurant. The door opens. She looks at the door.

"Emily!"

Nina is very surprised. Emily comes into the restaurant.

"Nina, I want to say 'sorry'," she says. "I made trouble for you. My son is a very bad man."

"What happened to your son?" asks Nina.

"He is in prison."

"Are you OK?" asks Nina.

"Oh yes. I feel better now. I don't have to steal things from shops. I don't have to do bad things. I feel good."

"I finish work in a few minutes," says Nina. "Would you like to go to a café for a cup of tea?"

"Oh yes, I would love to," says Emily.

"OK, please wait here," says Nina.

She goes into the staff room and takes her uniform off. She puts on a shirt and jeans. Then, she goes back into the restaurant, says 'goodbye' to the other staff, and opens the door. Emily and Nina walk to her car in the car park.

"Let's go to that nice café near the department store," says Nina.

They go to the café and enjoy talking about many things.

After that, Nina and Emily become good friends. Every day, Nina picks Emily up from the supermarket. Emily's bag is not so heavy. There is food in her bag. Only food. No DVDs, no shoes, no ties and no shirts.

THANK YOU

Thank you for reading Emily's Bag. (Word count: 5,236) We hope you enjoyed the story.

There are quizzes about this book on our free study site I Talk You Talk Press EXTRA. http://italk-youtalk.com

If you would like to read more graded readers, please visit our website http://www.italkyoutalk.com

Other Level 1 graded readers include
A Business Trip to New York
A Homestay in Auckland
A Trip to London
Dear Ellen
Haruna's Story Part 1
Haruna's Story Part 2
Haruna's Story Part 3
Ken's Story Part 1
Ken's Story Part 2
Life is Surprising!
Strange Stories
The Christmas Present
The Old Hospital
We Met Online

ABOUT THE AUTHOR

I Talk You Talk Press is a Japan-based publisher of language textbooks, graded readers and language learning/teaching resources.

Our team is made up of highly experienced language teachers and translators, who have all studied at least one additional language to an advanced level.

This experience enables us to design our materials from the perspective of both the teacher and the learner. We consult with both teachers and language learners when designing our textbooks and graded readers, and test our materials extensively in the classroom before publication.

We are a fast-growing press, and currently publish graded readers for learners of English. We publish new graded readers monthly.